If Animals Came to S

SCHOOL

What would happen if animals came to school?

If monkeys came to school,
art class would be messy.

But recess would be fun!

If elephants came to school,
story time would be crowded.

But lining up would be fun!

If alligators came to school,
lunchtime would be busy.

But field trips would be fun!

If turtles came to school,
races would be slow.

But playing hide-and-seek would be fun!

If camels came to school,
going to the library would be a problem.

But leaving the library would be fun!

If kangaroos came to school,
music class would be noisy.

But clean-up time would be fun!

Do animals come to your school?

Sometimes they come to mine!